A Special Gift

TO:

FROM:

DATE:

Precious ARE THE Promises

Paintings by Ron DiCianni

CONTENTS

CHAPTER ONE

GOD'S PROMISES OF BLESSING

The Lord gives

his blessing

when he finds

the vessel empty.

THOMAS Á KEMPIS

ho may go up on the mountain of the LORD? Who may stand in his holy Temple? Only those with clean hands and pure hearts, who have not worshiped idols, who have not made promises in the name of a false god. They will receive a blessing from the LORD; the God who saves them will declare them right.

PSALM 24:3-6, NCV

Blessed be the God and Father of our LORD Jesus Christ, who hath blessed us with all spiritual blessings in heavenly places in Christ.

EPHESIANS 1:3, KJV

Blessed is the man who trusts in the LORD, whose confidence is in him. He will be like a tree planted by the water that sends out its roots by the stream. It does not fear when heat comes; its leaves are always green. It has no worries in a year of drought and never fails to bear fruit.

JEREMIAH 17:7-8, NIV

I will bless them and the places surrounding my hill. I will send down showers in season; there will be showers of blessing.

EZEKIEL 34:26, NIV

We have all benefited from the rich blessing heaped upon us!

JOHN 1:16, TLB

For I will pour water on him who is thirsty, and floods on the dry ground; I will pour my Spirit on your descendents, and My blessing on your offspring.

ISAIAH 44:3, NKJV

Blessed are the poor in spirit: for theirs is the kingdom of heaven.

Blessed are they that mourn: for they shall be comforted.

Blessed are the meek: for they shall inherit the earth.

Blessed are they which hunger and thirst after righteousness: for they shall be filled.

Blessed are the merciful: for they shall obtain mercy.

Blessed are the pure in heart: for they shall see God.

Blessed are the peacemakers: for they shall be called the children of God.

Blessed are they which are persecuted because of righteousness' sake: for theirs is the kingdom of heaven.

MATTHEW 5:3-10, KJV

CHAPTER TWO

GOD'S PROMISES OF COMPASSION

et the LORD longs to be gracious to you; he rises to show you compassion. For the LORD is a God of justice. Blessed are all who wait for him!

ISAIAH 30:18, NIV

The LORD said, "I will make all My goodness pass before you, and I will proclaim the name of the LORD before you. I will be gracious to whom I will be gracious, and I will have compassion on whom I will have compassion."

EXODUS 33:19, NKJV

Bless the LORD, O my soul, and forget none of His benefits; Who pardons all your iniquities; Who heals all your diseases; Who redeems your life from the pit; Who crowns you with loving kindness and compassion; Who satisfies your years with good things, So that your youth is renewed like the eagle.

PSALM 103:2–5, NASB

The LORD is gracious and righteous; our God is full of compassion.

PSALM 116:5, NIV

For the LORD will judge His people and He will have compassion on his servants.

PSALM 135:14, NKJV

Can a woman forget her nursing child and have no compassion on the son of her womb? Even these may forget, but I will not forget you.

ISAIAH 49:15, NASB

"Though the mountains be shaken and the hills be removed, yet my unfailing love for you will not be shaken nor my covenant of peace be removed," says the LORD, who has compassion on you.

ISAIAH 54:10, NIV

Jesus called his disciples unto him and said, "I have compassion for the multitude, because they continue with me now three days, and have nothing to eat. I will not send them away fasting, lest they faint in the way."

MATTHEW 15:32, KJV

Praise be to the God and Father of our LORD Jesus Christ, the Father of compassion and the God of all comfort.

2 CORINTHIANS 1:3, NIV

ecause of the Lord's great love we are not consumed, for his compassions never fail. They are new every morning; great is your faithfulness.

LAMENTATIONS 3:22-23 NIV

When they cried out to you again, you heard from heaven, and in your compassion you delivered them time after time.

NEHEMIAH 9:28 NIV

As a father has compassion on his children, so the Lord has compassion on those who fear him.

PSALM 103:13 NIV

Shout for joy, O heavens; rejoice, O earth; burst into song, O mountains! For the Lord comforts his people and will have compassion on his afflicted ones.

ISAIAH 49:13 NIV

"For a brief moment I abandoned you, but with deep compassion I will bring you back. In a surge of anger I hid my face from you for a moment, but with everlasting kindness I will have compassion on you," says the Lord your Redeemer.

ISAIAH 54:7-8 NIV

I will betroth you to me forever; I will betroth you in righteousness and justice, in love and compassion.

HOSEA 2:19 NIV

Have mercy on me, O God, according to your unfailing love; according to your great compassion blot out my transgressions.

PSALM 51:1 NIV

Rend your heart and not your garments. Return to the Lord your God, for he is gracious and compassionate, slow to anger and abounding in love, and he relents from sending calamity.

JOEL 2:13 NIV

He says to Moses, "I will have mercy on whom I have mercy, and I will have compassion on whom I have compassion."

ROMANS 9:15 NIV

GOD'S PROMISES OF COURAGE

 praise God for his word. I trust God, so I am not afraid.
What can human beings do to me?

PSALM 56:4, NCV

He will cover you with His pinions, and under His wings
you may seek refuge; His faithfulness is a shield and
bulwark. You will not be afraid of the terror by night, or
of the arrow that flies by day.

PSALM 91:4-5, NASB

Then you will walk safely in your way, and your foot will
not stumble. When you lie down, you will not be afraid;
yes, you will lie down and your sleep will be sweet. Do
not be afraid of sudden terror, nor of trouble from the
wicked when it comes; for the LORD will be your confidence, and will keep your foot from being caught.

PROVERBS 3:23-26, NKJV

See, God has come to save me! I will trust and not
be afraid, for the Lord is my strength and song; he is
my salvation.

ISAIAH 12:2, TLB

Say to those with fearful hearts, "Be strong, do not fear;
your God will come, he will come with vengeance;
with divine retribution he will come to save you."

ISAIAH 35:4, NIV.

For Jehovah is my refuge! I choose the God above all
gods to shelter me. How then can evil overtake me or
any plague come near? For he orders his angels to protect
you wherever you go.

PSALM 91:9-11, TLB

Fear thou not; for I am with thee; be not dismayed;
for I am thy God; I will strengthen thee; yea, I will help
thee; yea, I will uphold thee with the right hand of my
righteousness.

ISAIAH 41:10, KJV

For I am the LORD, your God, who takes hold of your
right hand and says to you, 'Do not fear; I will help you.'

ISAIAH 41:13, NIV

Don't be afraid, because you will not be ashamed.
Don't be embarrassed, because you will not be disgraced.

ISAIAH 54:4, NCV

CHAPTER FOUR

GOD'S PROMISES OF FORGIVENESS

Forgiveness is our

deepest need and our

highest achievement.

HORACE BUSHNELL

or as high as the heavens are above the earth, so great is His lovingkindness toward those who fear Him. As far as the east is from the west, so far has He removed our transgressions from us.

PSALM 103:11-12, NASB

If My people who are called by My name will humble themselves, and pray and seek My face, and turn from their wicked ways, then I will hear from heaven, and will forgive their sin and will heal their land.

2 CHRONICLES 7:14, NKJV

Lord, if you keep in mind our sins then who can ever get an answer to his prayers? But you forgive! What an awesome thing this is!

PSALM 130:3-4, TLB

If you forgive others for their sins, your Father in heaven will also forgive you for your sins.

MATTHEW 6:14, NCV

Jesus said, "Father, forgive them, for they do not know what they are doing."

LUKE 23:34, NIV

Jesus is the One whom God raised to be on his right side, as Leader and Savior. Through him, all people could change their hearts and lives and have their sins forgiven.

ACTS 5:31, NCV

For I will forgive their wickedness and will remember their sins no more.

HEBREWS 8:12, NIV

If we confess our sins, He is faithful and righteous to forgive us our sins and to cleanse us from all unrighteousness.

1 JOHN 1:9, NASB

In him we have redemption through his blood, the forgiveness of sins, in accordance with the riches of God's grace.

EPHESIANS 1:7, NIV

I will cleanse them from all the sin they have committed against me and will forgive all their sins of rebellion against me.

JEREMIAH 33:8, NIV

GOD'S PROMISES OF FAITHFULNESS

emember this—the wrong desires that come into your life aren't anything new and different. Many others have faced exactly the same problems before you. And no temptation is irresistible. You can trust God to keep the temptation from becoming so strong that you can't stand up against it, for he has promised this and will do what he says. He will show you how to escape temptation's power so that you can bear up patiently against it.

1 CORINTHIANS 10:13, TLB

Your kingdom will go on and on, and you will rule forever. The LORD will keep all his promises; he is loyal to all he has made.

PSALM 145:13, NKJV

Know therefore that the LORD your God is God; he is the faithful God, keeping his covenant of love to a thousand generations of those who love him and keep his commands.

DEUTERONOMY 7:9, NIV

For the word of the LORD is right; and all his works are done in truth.

PSALM 33:4, KJV

The Rock! His work is perfect, for all His ways are just; a God of faithfulness and without injustice, righteous and upright is He.

DEUTERONOMY 32:4, NASB

LORD, you are loyal to those who are loyal, and you are good to those who are good.

2 SAMUEL 22:26, NCV

For great is his love toward us, and the faithfulness of the LORD endures forever. Praise the LORD.

PSALM 117:2, NIV

O LORD, I will honor and praise your name, for you are my God; you do such wonderful things! You planned them long ago, and now you have accomplished them, just as you said!

ISAIAH 25:1, TLB

But the LORD is faithful, who shall stablish you, and keep you from evil.

2 THESSALONIANS 3:3, KJV

But Christ was faithful as a Son over His house whose house we are, if we hold fast our confidence and the boast of our hope firm until the end.

HEBREWS 3:6, NASB

CHAPTER SIX

GOD'S PROMISES OF GRACE

od makes people right with himself through their faith in Jesus Christ. This is true for all who believe in Christ, because all people are the same: All have sinned and are not good enough for God's glory, and all need to be made right with God by his grace, which is a free gift.

ROMANS 3:22-24, NCV

The sin of this one man, Adam, caused death to be king over all, but all who will take God's gift of forgiveness and acquittal of kings of life because of this one man, Jesus Christ.

ROMANS 5:17, TLB

Where sin abounded, grace did much more abound.

ROMANS 5:20, KJV

To each one of us grace was given according to the measure of Christ's gift.

EPHESIANS 4:7, NKJV

My grace is sufficient for thee: for my strength is made perfect in weakness.

2 CORINTHIANS 12:9, KJV

It is the same now. There are a few people that God has chosen by his grace. And if he chose them by grace, it is not for the things they have done. If they could be made God's people by what they did, God's gift of grace would not really be a gift.

ROMANS 11:5-6, NCV

But God, being rich in mercy, because of His great love with which He loved us, even when we were dead in our transgressions, made us alive together with Christ (by grace you have been saved), and raised us up with Him, and seated us with Him in the heavenly places, in Christ Jesus. For by grace you have been saved through faith; and that not of yourselves, it is the gift of God; not as a result of works, that no one should boast.

EPHESIANS 2:4-5, 8-9, NASB

He saved us, not because of righteous things we had done, but because of his mercy. He saved us through the washing of rebirth and renewal by the Holy Spirit, whom he poured out on us generously through Jesus Christ our Savior, so that, having been justified by his grace, we might become heirs having the hope of eternal life.

TITUS 3:5-7, NIV

CHAPTER
SEVEN

GOD'S PROMISES OF HEALING

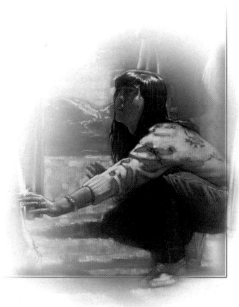

When praying for healing, ask
great things of God and expect great
things from God. But let us seek
for the healing that really matters,
the healing of the heart, enabling
us to trust God simply, face God
honestly, and live triumphantly.

ARLO F. NEWELL

ut he took our suffering on him and felt our pain for us. We saw his suffering and thought God was punishing him. But he was wounded for the wrong we did; he was crushed for the evil we did. The punishment, which made us well, was given to him, and we are healed because of his wounds.

ISAIAH 53:4-5, NCV

He heals the brokenhearted, binding up their wounds.

PSALM 147:3, TLB

Then your light will shine like the dawn, and your wounds will quickly heal. Your God will walk before you, and the glory of the LORD will protect you from behind.

ISAIAH 58:8, NCV

I will bring [them] health and healing, and I will heal them; and I will reveal to them an abundance of peace and truth.

JEREMIAH 33:6, NASB

They cried out the LORD in their trouble, and He saved them out of their distresses. He sent His word and healed them, and delivered them from their destructions.

PSALM 107:19-20, NKJV

He called his twelve disciples to him and gave them authority to drive out evil spirits and to heal every disease and sickness.

MATTHEW 10:1, NIV

He personally carried the load of our sins in his own body when he died on the cross, so that we can be finished with sin and live a good life from now on. For his wounds have healed ours!

1 PETER 2:24, TLB

Great multitudes came unto him, having with them those that were lame, blind, dumb, maimed, and many others, and cast them down at Jesus' feet; and he healed them.

MATTHEW 15:30, KJV

And everywhere he went—into towns, cities, or countryside—the people brought the sick to the marketplaces. They begged him to let them touch just the edge of his coat, and all who touched it were healed.

MARK 6:56, NCV

Therefore confess your sins to each other and pray for each other so that you may be healed. The prayer of a righteous man is powerful and effective.

JAMES 5:16, NIV

GOD'S PROMISES OF GUIDANCE

If I rise on the wings of the dawn, if I settle on the far side of the sea, even there your hand will guide me, your right hand will hold me fast.

PSALM 139:9-10, NIV

You have led the people you redeemed. But in your lovingkindness you have guided them wonderfully to your holy land.

EXODUS 15:13, TLB

He restoreth my soul: he leadeth me in the paths of righteousness for his name's sake.

PSALM 23:3, KJV

The LORD will always lead you. He will satisfy your needs in dry lands and will give strength to your bones. You will be like a garden that has much water, like a spring that never runs dry.

ISAIAH 58:11, NCV

The meek will he guide in judgment; and the meek will he teach his way.

PSALM 25:9, KJV

For this great God is our God forever and ever. He will be our guide until we die.

PSALM 48:14, TLB

This is what the LORD, who saves you, the Holy One of Israel, says: 'I am the LORD your God, who teaches you what is good, who leads you in the way you should go.

ISAIAH 48:17, NCV

But when He, the Spirit of truth, comes, He will guide you into all truth. He will not speak on His own initiative; but whatever He hears, He will speak; and He will disclose to you what is to come.

JOHN 16:13, NASB

In his heart a man plans his course, but the LORD determines his steps.

PROVERBS 16:9, NIV

CHAPTER NINE

GOD'S PROMISES OF ETERNAL LIFE

How completely satisfying to turn from our limitations to a God who has none. Eternal years lie in his heart. For him time does not pass, it remains. And those who are in Christ share with him all the riches of limitless time and endless years.

A.W. TOZER

veryone who has left houses or brothers or sisters or father or mother or children or fields for my sake will receive a hundred times as much and will inherit eternal life.

MATTHEW 19:29, NIV

And as Moses lifted up the serpent in the wilderness, even so must the Son of man be lifted up: That whosoever believeth in him should not perish, but have eternal life. For God so loved the world that he gave his only begotten son, that whosoever believeth in him should not perish, but have eternal life.

JOHN 3:14-16, KJV

Truly, truly, I say to you, he who hears My word, and believes Him who sent Me, has eternal life, and does not come into judgment, but has passed out of death into life.

JOHN 5:24, NASB

These things Jesus spoke; and lifting up His eyes to heaven, He said, "Father, the hour has come; glorify Thy Son, that the Son may glorify Thee, even as Thou gavest Him authority over all mankind, that to all whom Thou hast given Him, He may give eternal life."

JOHN 17:1-3, NASB

My sheep listen to my voice; I know them, and they follow me. I give them eternal life, and they will never die; and no one can steal them out of my hand.

JOHN 10:27-28, NCV

Some people by always continuing to do good, live for God's glory, for honor, and for life that has no end. God will give them life forever.

ROMANS 2:7, NCV

This is the promise that he hath promised us, even eternal life.

1 JOHN 2:25, KJV

And this is the record, that God hath given to us eternal life, and this life is in his Son.

1 JOHN 5:11, KJV

This is the will of Him who sent Me, that everyone who sees the Son and believes in Him may have everlasting life; and I will raise him up at the last day.

JOHN 6:40, NKJV

CHAPTER TEN

GOD'S PROMISES THAT HE WILL LISTEN TO US

he Lord has heard my cry for mercy; the Lord accepts my prayer.

> PSALM 6:9, NIV

For then you will have your delight in the Almighty, and lift up your face to God. You will make your prayer to Him and He will hear you.

> JOB 22:26-27, NKJV

I cried unto the LORD with my voice, and he heard me out of his holy hill.

> PSALM 3:4, KJV

Know that the LORD has set apart the godly man for Himself; the LORD hears when I call to Him.

> PSALM 4:3, NASB

I sought the LORD, and he heard me; and delivered me from all my fears.

> PSALM 34:4, KJV

I waited patiently for God to help me; then he listened and heard my cry.

PSALM 40:1, TLB

But as for me, I watch in hope for the LORD, I wait for God my Savior; my God will hear me.

MICAH 7:7, NIV

O Lord, you are so good and kind, so ready to forgive; so full of mercy for all who ask your aid. Listen closely to my prayer, O God. Hear my urgent cry. I will call to you whenever trouble strikes, and you will help me.

PSALM 86:5-7, TLB

I love the LORD, because He hears my prayers and my supplications.

PSALM 116:1, NASB

Hear my voice in accordance with your love; preserve my life, O LORD, according to your laws.

PSALM 119:149, NIV

When I was in trouble, I called to the LORD, and he answered me.

PSALM 120:1, NCV

CHAPTER ELEVEN

GOD'S PROMISES OF HEAVEN

Anyone can devise a plan by which good people may go to heaven. Only God could devise a plan whereby sinners, who are his enemies, can go there.

LEWIS SPERRY CHAFER

hou shalt guide me with the counsel, and afterward receive me to glory. Whom have I in Heaven but thee? And there is none upon earth that I desire beside thee.

PSALM 73:24-25, KJV

Dominion and awe belong to Him who establishes peace in His heights.

JOB 25:2, NASB

But our homeland is in heaven, where our Savior the Lord Jesus Christ is; and we are looking forward to his return from there. When he comes back he will take these dying bodies of ours and change them into glorious bodies like his own, using the same mighty power that he will use to conquer all else everywhere.

PHILIPPIANS 3:20-21, TLB

But the Lord's love for those who respect him continues forever and ever, and his goodness continues to their grandchildren and to those who keep his agreement and who remember to obey his orders.

PSALM 103:17-19, NCV

You should not be happy because the spirits obey you but because your names are written in heaven.

LUKE 10:20, NCV

Blessed are those who are persecuted because of righteousness, for theirs is the kingdom of heaven. Blessed are you when people insult you, persecute you and falsely say all kinds of evil against you because of me. Rejoice and be glad, because great is your reward in heaven, for in the same way they persecuted the prophets who were before you.

MATTHEW 5:10-12, NIV

Lay up for yourselves treasures in heaven, where neither moth nor rust doth corrupt, and where thieves do not break through nor steal.

MATTHEW 6:20, KJV

Not everyone who says to me, "LORD, LORD," shall enter the kingdom of heaven, but only he who does the will of my Father who is in heaven.

MATTHEW 7:21, NKJV

I say to you, that many shall come from east and west, and recline at the table with Abraham, and Isaac, and Jacob, in the kingdom of heaven.

MATTHEW 8:11, NASB

CHAPTER TWELVE

GOD'S PROMISES OF THE HOLY SPIRIT

he Counselor, the Holy Spirit, whom the Father will send in my name, will teach you all things and will remind you of everything I have said to you.

JOHN 14:26, NIV

If you then, being evil, know how to give good gifts to your children, how much more shall your heavenly Father give the Holy Spirit to those who ask him?

LUKE 11:13, NASB

I will send you the comforter—the Holy Spirit, the source of all truth. He will come to you from the Father and will tell you all about me.

JOHN 15:26, TLB

You will receive power when the Holy Spirit has come upon you; and you shall be My witness both in Jeruslem, and Samaria, and even to the remotest part of the earth.

ACTS 2:38, NCV

It is the Spirit that gives life. The flesh doesn't give life. The words I told you are spirit, and they give life.

JOHN 6:63, NCV

Do you not know that your body is a temple of the Holy Spirit, who is in you, whom you have received from God? You are not your own; you were bought at a price. Therefore honor God with your body.

1 CORINTHIANS 6:19-20, NIV

Not only that, but we also glory in tribulations, knowing that tribulation produces perseverance; and perseverance, character, and character, hope. Now hope does not disappoint, because the love of God has been poured out in our hearts by the Holy Spirit who was given to us.

ROMANS 5:3-5, NKJV

But now in Christ Jesus, you who were far away from God are brought near through the blood of Christ's death. Christ himself is our peace. He made both Jewish people and those who are not Jews one people.

EPHESIANS 1:13-14, NCV

Peter said to them, "change your hearts and your lives and be baptized, each one of you, in the name of Jesus Christ for the forgiveness of your sins. And you will receive the gift of the Holy Spirit."

ACTS 2:38, NCV

CHAPTER THIRTEEN

GOD'S PROMISES OF LOVE

There is nothing we can do

to make God love us more!

There is nothing we can do

to make Him love us less!

His love is unconditional,

impartial, everlasting, infinite,

perfect! God is love!

e know how much God loves us because we have felt his love and because we believe him when he tells us that he loves us dearly. God is love, and anyone who lives in love is living with God and God is living in him.

1 JOHN 4:16, TLB

Know therefore that the LORD your God, He is God; the faithful God, who keeps His covenant and His loving-kindness to a thousand generations with those who love Him and keep His commandments.

DEUTERONOMY 7:9, NASB

Give thanks unto the LORD; for he is good; his mercy endures forever.

1 CHRONICLES 16:34, KJV

Surely goodness and mercy shall follow me all the days of my life; and I will dwell in the house of the LORD forever.

PSALM 23:6, KJV

LORD, your love reaches to the heavens, your loyalty to the skies. God, your love is so precious! You protect people in the shadow of your wings.

PSALM 36:5, 7, NCV

The LORD will command His lovingkindness in the day-time; and His song will be with me in the night, a prayer to the God of my life.

PSALM 42:8, NASB

For as the heaven is high above the earth, so great is his mercy toward them that fear him.

PSALM 103:11, KJV

O Israel, hope in the LORD, for with the LORD there is mercy, and with Him is abundant redemption.

PSALM 130:7, NKJV

For the mountains may depart and the hills disappear, but my kindness shall not leave you. My promise of peace for you will never be broken, says the LORD who has mercy upon you.

ISAIAH 54:10, TLB

Just as it is written, "Things which eye has not seen and ear has not heard, and which have not entered the heart of man, all that God has prepared for those who love him."

1 CORINTHIANS 2:9, NASB

his hope will never disappoint us, because God has poured out his love to fill our hearts. He gave us his love through the Holy spirit, whom God has given to us.

ROMANS 5:5, NCV

See how very much our heavenly Father loves us, for he allows us to be called his children—think of it—and we really are!

1 JOHN 3:1, TLB

For I am persuaded, that neither death, nor life, nor angels, nor principalities, nor powers, nor things present, nor things to come, nor height, nor depth, nor any other creature, shall be able to separate us from the love of God, which is in Christ Jesus our Lord.

ROMANS 8:38-39, KJV

Love is patient, love is kind. It does not envy, it does not boast, it is not proud. It is not rude, it is not self-seeking, it is not easily angered, it keeps no record of wrongs. Love does not delight in evil but rejoices with the truth. It always protects, always trusts, always hopes, always perseveres. Love never fails.

1 CORINTHIANS 13:4-8, NIV

God shows his great love for us in this way: Christ died for us while we were still sinners.

ROMANS 5:8, NCV

Let the morning bring me word of your unfailing love, for I have put my trust in you. Show me the way I should go, for to you I lift up my soul.

PSALM 143:8 NIV

Many waters cannot quench love; rivers cannot wash it away. If one were to give all the wealth of his house for love, it would be utterly scorned.

SONG OF SOLOMON 8:7 NIV

That Christ may dwell in your hearts by faith; that ye, being rooted and grounded in love, May be able to comprehend with all saints what is the breadth, and length, and depth, and height; And to know the love of Christ, which passeth knowledge, that ye might be filled with all the fulness of God.

EPHESIANS 3:17-19 KJV

The earth is filled with your love, O Lord; teach me your decrees.

PSALM 119:64 NIV

CHAPTER FOURTEEN

GOD'S PROMISES OF HOPE

"or I know the plans I have for you," declares the Lord, "plans to prosper you and not to harm you, plans to give you hope and a future."

JEREMIAH 29:11, NIV

Then you would trust, because there is hope; and you would look around and rest securely.

JOB 11:18, NASB

The eye of the LORD is upon them that fear him, upon them that hope in his mercy.

PSALM 33:18, KJV

Let us hold unswervingly to the hope we profess, for he who promised is faithful.

HEBREWS 10:23, NIV

They that wait upon the LORD shall renew their strength; they shall mount up with wings as eagles; they shall run and not be weary; and they shall walk, and not faint.

ISAIAH 40:31, KJV

I pray for you Gentiles that God who gives you hope will keep you happy and full of peace as you believe in him. I pray that God will help you overflow with hope in him through the Holy Spirit's power within you.

ROMANS 15:13, TLB

I pray also that you will have greater understanding in your heart so you will know the hope to which he has called us and that you will know how rich and glorious are the blessings God has promised his holy people. And you will know that God's power is very great for us who believe.

EPHESIANS 1:18-19, NCV

All honor to God, the God and Father of our Lord Jesus Christ; for it is his boundless mercy that has given us the privilege of being born again, so that we are now members of God's own family.

1 PETER 1:3, TLB

Don't envy sinners, but always respect the LORD, then you will have hope for the future, and your wishes will come true.

PROVERBS 23: 17-18, NCV

he Spirit of the Sovereign Lord is on me, because the Lord has anointed me to preach good news to the poor. He has sent me to bind up the brokenhearted, to proclaim freedom for the captives and release from darkness for the prisoners, to proclaim the year of the Lord's favor and the day of vengeance of our God, to comfort all who mourn, and provide for those who grieve in Zion — to bestow on them a crown of beauty instead of ashes, the oil of gladness instead of mourning, and a garment of praise instead of a spirit of despair. They will be called oaks of righteousness, a planting of the Lord for the display of his splendor.

ISAIAH 61:1-3 NIV

You will be secure, because there is hope; you will look about you and take your rest in safety.

JOB 11:18 NIV

Then you will know that I am the Lord; those who hope in me will not be disappointed.

ISAIAH 49:23 NIV

Though he slay me, yet will I hope in him.

JOB 13:15 NIV

Find rest, O my soul, in God alone; my hope comes from him.

PSALM 62:5 NIV

No one whose hope is in you will ever be put to shame, but they will be put to shame who are treacherous without excuse.

PSALM 25:3 NIV

Why are you downcast, O my soul? Why so disturbed within me? Put your hope in God, for I will yet praise him, my Savior and my God.

PSALM 42:11 NIV

We wait for the blessed hope — the glorious appearing of our great God and Savior, Jesus Christ, who gave himself for us to redeem us from all wickedness and to purify for himself a people that are his very own, eager to do what is good.

TITUS 2:13-14 NIV

For thou art my hope, O Lord GOD: thou art my trust from my youth.

PSALM 71:5 KJV

There is surely a future hope for you, and your hope will not be cut off.

PROVERBS 23:18 NIV

Everything that was written in the past was written to teach us, so that through endurance and the encouragement of the Scriptures we might have hope.

ROMANS 15:4 NIV

CHAPTER
FIFTEEN

GOD'S PROMISES OF PEACE

God takes life's

pieces and gives

us unbroken peace.

W. D. GOUGH

eace I leave with you, my peace I give unto you: not as the world giveth, give I unto you. Let not your heart be troubled, neither let it be afraid.

JOHN 14:27, KJV

The LORD will give strength to His people; the LORD will bless His people with peace.

PSALM 29:11, NASB

The meek will inherit the earth; and shall delight themselves in the abundance of peace.

PSALM 37:11, KJV

When a man's ways are pleasing to the LORD, he makes even his enemies live at peace with him.

PROVERBS 16:7, NIV

You will keep him in perfect peace, whose mind is stayed on You, because he trusts in You.

ISAIAH 26:3, NKJV

I have told you all this so that you will have peace of heart and mind. Here on earth you will have many trials and sorrows; but cheer up, for I have overcome the world.

JOHN 16:33, TLB

I will lie down and sleep in peace, for you alone, O LORD, make me dwell in safety.

PSALM 4:8, NIV

For God is not the author of confusion, but of peace.

1 CORINTHIANS 14:33, KJV

Therefore having been justified by faith, we have peace with God through our Lord Jesus Christ.

ROMANS 5:1, NASB

Don't worry about anything; instead, pray about everything; tell God your needs and don't forget to thank him for his answers. If you do this you will experience God's peace, which is far more wonderful than the human mind can understand. His peace will keep your thoughts and your hearts quiet and at rest as you trust in Christ Jesus.

PHILIPPIANS 4:6-7, TLB

Those who walk uprightly enter into peace.

ISAIAH 57:2 NIV

A heart at peace gives life to the body.

PROVERBS 14:30 NIV

iscipline your son, and he will give you peace; he will bring delight to your soul.

PROVERBS 29:17 NIV

For unto us a child is born, unto us a son is given: and the government shall be upon his shoulder: and his name shall be called Wonderful, Counseller, The mighty God, The everlasting Father, The Prince of Peace.

ISAIAH 9:6 KJV

The work of righteousness shall be peace; and the effect of righteousness quietness and assurance for ever.

ISAIAH 32:17 KJV

Moreover I will make a covenant of peace with them; it shall be an everlasting covenant with them: and I will place them, and multiply them, and will set my sanctuary in the midst of them for evermore.

EZEKIEL 37:26 KJV

And suddenly there was with the angel a multitude of the heavenly host praising God, and saying, Glory to God in the highest, and on earth peace, good will toward men.

LUKE 2:13-14 KJV

The mind of sinful man is death, but the mind controlled by the Spirit is life and peace.

ROMANS 8:6 NIV

Now in Christ Jesus you who once were far away have been brought near through the blood of Christ. For he himself is our peace, who has made the two one and has destroyed the barrier, the dividing wall of hostility, by abolishing in his flesh the law with its commandments and regulations. His purpose was to create in himself one new man out of the two, thus making peace.

EPHESIANS 2:13-15 NIV

Let the peace of Christ rule in your hearts, since as members of one body you were called to peace.

COLOSSIANS 3:15 NIV

No discipline seems pleasant at the time, but painful. Later on, however, it produces a harvest of righteousness and peace for those who have been trained by it.

HEBREWS 12:11 NIV

Peacemakers who sow in peace raise a harvest of righteousness.

JAMES 3:18 NIV

CHAPTER SIXTEEN

GOD'S PROMISES OF JOY

ou have made known to me the path of life; you will fill me with joy in your presence, with eternal pleasures at your right hand.

PSALM 16:11, NIV

The LORD hath done great things for us; whereof we are glad.

PSALM 126:3, KJV

God's laws are perfect. They protect us, make us wise, and give us joy and light.

PSALM 19:7-8, TLB

The ransomed of the LORD will return. They will enter Zion with singing; everlasting joy will crown their heads. Gladness and joy will overtake them, and sorrow and sighing will flee away.

ISAIAH 35:10, NIV

You will live in joy and peace. The mountains and hills, the trees of the field—all the world around you—will rejoice.

ISAIAH 55:12, TLB

I have obeyed my Father's commands, and I remain in his love. In the same way, if you obey my commands, you will remain in my love. I have told you these things so that you can have the same joy I have and so that your joy will be the fullest possible joy.

JOHN 15:10-11, NCV

Instead of your shame you shall have double honor, and instead of confusion they shall rejoice in their portion. Therefore in their land they shall possess double; everlasting joy shall be theirs.

ISAIAH 61:7, NKJV

Then maidens will dance and be glad, young men and old as well. I will turn their mourning into gladness; I will give them comfort and joy instead of sorrow.

JEREMIAH 31:13, NIV

When my anxious thoughts multiply within me. Thy consolations delight my soul.

PSALM 94:19, NASB

They that sow in tears shall reap in joy.

PSALM 126:5, KJV

ow you are sad, but I will see you again and you will be happy, and no one will take away your joy. In that day you will not ask me for anything. I tell you the truth, my Father will give you anything you ask for in my name. Until now you have not asked for anything in my name. Ask and you will receive, so that your joy will be the fullest possible joy.

JOHN 16:22-24, NCV

For his anger endureth but a moment; in his favour is life: weeping may endure for a night, but joy cometh in the morning.

PSALM 30:5 KJV

He will yet fill your mouth with laughter and your lips with shouts of joy.

JOB 8:21 NIV

You have filled my heart with greater joy than when their grain and new wine abound.

PSALM 4:7 NIV

But let all those that put their trust in thee rejoice: let them ever shout for joy, because thou defendest them: let them also that love thy name be joyful in thee.

PSALM 5:11 KJV

You turned my wailing into dancing; you removed my sackcloth and clothed me with joy, that my heart may sing to you and not be silent. O Lord my God, I will give you thanks forever.

PSALM 30:11-12 NIV

Let the righteous be glad; let them rejoice before God: yea, let them exceedingly rejoice.

PSALM 68:3 KJV

You make me glad by your deeds, O Lord; I sing for joy at the works of your hands.

PSALM 92:4

Light is shed upon the righteous and joy on the upright in heart.

PSALM 97:11 NIV

He brought forth his people with joy, and his chosen with gladness:

PSALM105:43 KJV

A cheerful look brings joy to the heart, and good news gives health to the bones.

PROVERBS 15:30 NIV

CHAPTER
SEVENTEEN

GOD'S PROMISES OF SALVATION

It is not our hold on

Christ that saves us,

but his hold on us!

CHARLES H. SPURGEON

f you confess with your mouth Jesus as Lord, and believe in your heart that God raised Him from the dead, you shall be saved; for with the heart man believes, resulting in righteousness, and with the mouth he confesses, resulting in salvation.

ROMANS 10:9-10, NASB

For God did not send his Son into the world to condemn the world, but to save the world through him.

JOHN 3:17, NIV

But God will redeem my soul from the power the grave; for He shall receive me.

PSALM 49:15, KJV

The LORD is pleased with is people; he saves the humble.

PSALM 149:4, NCV

I, even I, am the LORD, and beside me there is no savior.

ISAIAH 43:11, KJV

Look to Me, and be saved, all you ends of the earth! For I am God, and there is no other.

ISAIAH 45:22, NKJV

She will give birth to a son, and you are to give him the
name Jesus, because he will save his people from their sins.

MATTHEW 1:21, NIV

I stand silently before the LORD, waiting for him to
rescue me, for salvation comes from him alone. Yes, he
alone is my Rock, my rescuer, defense and fortress.

PSALM 62:1 2, TLB

They replied, "Believe in the LORD Jesus, and you will
be saved—you and your household."

ACTS 16:31, NIV

I am not ashamed of the gospel, because it is the power
of God for the salvation of everyone who believes.

ROMANS 1:16, NIV

For by grace are ye saved through faith; and that not of
yourselves: it is the gift of God.

EPHESIANS 2:8, KJV

GOD'S PROMISES OF JUSTICE

on't you think that God will surely give justice to his people who plead with him day and night? Yes! He will answer them quickly! But the question is: When I, the Messiah return, how many will I find who have faith and are praying?

LUKE 18:7-8, TLB

The LORD is known by the judgment He executes; the wicked is snared in the work of his own hands.

PSALM 9:16, NKJV

For the LORD is righteous; He loves righteousness; the upright will behold His face.

PSALM 11:7, NASB

The LORD executed righteousness and justice for all that are oppressed.

PSALM 103:6, KJV

I know that the LORD will get justice for the poor and will defend the needy in court.

PSALM 140:12, NCV

A bruised reed he will not break, and a smoldering wick he will not snuff out. In faithfulness he will bring forth justice; he will not falter or be discouraged till he establishes justice on earth.

ISAIAH 42:3-4, NIV

For he has set a day for justly judging the world by the man he has appointed, and has pointed him out by bringing him back to life again.

ACTS 17:31, TLB

He shall judge the world in righteousness, he shall minister judgment to the people in uprightness.

PSALM 9:8, KJV

God gave him as a way to forgive sin through faith in the blood of Jesus' death. This showed that God always does what is right and fair, as in the past when he was patient and did not punish people for their sins.

ROMANS 3:25, NCV

CHAPTER NINETEEN

GOD'S PROMISES OF MERCY

His mercy extends to those who fear him, from generation to generation.

LUKE 1:50, NIV

For the LORD your God is a compassionate God; He will not fail you nor destroy you nor forget the covenant with your fathers which He swore to them.

DEUTERONOMY 4:31, NASB

There is no God like you. You forgive those who are guilty of sin; you don't look at the sins of your people who are left alive. You will not stay angry forever, because you enjoy being kind.

MICAH 7:18, NCV

So then He has mercy on whom He desires, and He hardens whom He desires.

ROMANS 9:18, NASB

But because of his great love for us, God, who is rich in mercy, made us alive with Christ even when we were dead in transgressions.

EPHESIANS 2:4-5, NIV

Blessed are the merciful, for they shall be shown mercy.

MATTHEW 5:7, KJV

But when the kindness and love of God our Savior was shown, he saved us because of his mercy. It was not because of good deeds we did to be right with him. He saved us through the washing that made us new people through the Holy Spirit.

TITUS 3:4-5, NCV

It was necessary for Jesus to be like us, his brothers, so that he could be our merciful and faithful High Priest before God, a Priest who would be both merciful to us and faithful to God in dealing with the sins of the people.

HEBREWS 2:17, TLB

Let us then approach the throne of grace with confidence, so that we may receive mercy and find grace to help us in our time of need.

HEBREWS 4:16, NIV

For there will be no mercy to those who have shown no mercy. But if you have been merciful, then God's mercy toward you will win out over his judgment against you.

JAMES 2:13, TLB

CHAPTER TWENTY

GOD'S PROMISES OF PROTECTION

Security is not found in the things our eye can see or hand can touch. True security is found only in the invisible, unseen. Our security is in God alone.

he LORD is my shepherd; I shall not want. He maketh me to lie down in green pastures, he leadeth me beside the still waters. He restoreth my soul: he leadeth me in the paths of righteousness for his name's sake. Yea, though I walk through the valley of the shadow of death, I swill fear no evil, for thou are with me; thy rod and thy staff they comfort me. Thou preparest a table before me in the presence of mine enemies; thou anointest my head with oil; my cup runneth over. Surely goodness and mercy shall follow me all the days of my life; and I will dwell in the house of the LORD forever.

PSALM 23:1-6, KJV

You are my hiding place; you will protect me from trouble and surround me with songs of deliverance.

PSALM 32:7, NIV

The LORD says, "Whoever loves me, I will save. I will protect those who know me."

PSALM 91:14, NCV

I do not pray that You should take them out of the world, but that You should keep them from the evil one.

JOHN 17:15, NKJV

But the Lord is faithful, and He will strengthen and protect you from the evil one.

2 THESSALONIANS 3:3, NASB

Remain in me, and I will remain in you. A branch cannot produce fruit alone but must remain in the vine. In the same way, you cannot produce fruit alone but must remain in me.

JOHN 15:4, NCV

Listen! The virgin shall conceive a child! She shall give birth to a Son, and he shall be called 'Emmanuel' (meaning 'God is with us').

MATTHEW 1:23, TLB

And lo I am with you always, even to the end of the world.

MATTHEW 28:20, KJV

No man shall be able to stand before you all the days of your life; as I was with Moses, so I will be with you. I will not leave you nor forsake you.

JOSHUA 1:5, NKJV

Be strong and brave. Do not be afraid of them and don't be frightened, because the LORD your God will go with you. He will not leave you or forget you.

DEUTERONOMY 31:6, NCV

CHAPTER
TWENTY-TWO

GOD'S PROMISES OF STRENGTH

When God is our

strength, it is strength

indeed. When our

strength is our own,

it is only weakness.

AUGUSTINE

e gives strength to those who are tired and more power to those who are weak. But the people who trust the Lord will become strong again. They will rise up as an eagle in the sky; they will run and not need rest; they will walk and not become tired.

ISAIAH 40:29, 31, NCV

It is God who arms me with strength and makes my way perfect.

PSALM 18:32, NIV

The LORD is my strength and my shield; my heart trusts in him, and I am helped. My heart leaps for joy and I will give thanks to him in song. The LORD is the strength of his people, a fortress of salvation for his anointed one.

PSALM 28:7-8, NIV

But as for me, I shall sing of Thy strength; yes, I shall joyfully sing of Thy lovingkindness in the morning, for Thou hast been my stronghold, and a refuge in the day of my distress. O my strength, I will sing praises to Thee; for God is my stronghold, the God who shows me loving kindness.

PSALM 59:16-17, NASB

O God, You are more awesome than Your holy places. The God of Israel is He who gives strength and power to His people. Blessed be God!

PSALM 68:35, NKJV

My flesh and my heart may fail, but God is the strength of my heart and my portion forever.

PSALM 73:26, NIV

The LORD is like a strong tower; those who do right can run to him for safety.

PROVERBS 18:10, NCV

He said to me, "My grace is sufficient for you, for my power is made perfect in weakness." Therefore I will boast all the more gladly about my weaknesses, so that Christ's power may rest on me.

2 CORINTHIANS 12:9, NIV

I can do all things through Christ who strengthens me.

PHILIPPIANS 4:13, NKJV

GOD'S PROMISES OF PROVISION

nd my God shall supply all your needs according to His riches in glory in Christ Jesus.

PHILIPPIANS 4:19, NASB

Therefore I tell you, do not worry about your life, what you will eat or drink; or about your body, what you will wear. Is not life more important than food, and the body more important than clothes? Look at the birds of the air; they do not sow or reap or store away in barns, and yet your heavenly Father feeds them. Are you not much more valuable than they? Who of you by worrying can add a single hour to his life?

And why do you worry about clothes? See how the lilies of the field grow. They do not labor or spin. Yet I tell you that not even Solomon in all his splendor was dressed like one of these. If that is how God clothes the grass of the field, which is here today and tomorrow is thrown into the fire, will he not much more clothe you, O you of little faith? So do not worry, saying, "What shall we eat?" or "What shall we drink?" or "What shall we wear?" For the pagans run after all these things, and your heavenly Father knows that you need them. But seek first his kingdom and his righteousness, and all these things will be given to you as well.

MATTHEW 6:25-33, NIV

Bring all the tithes into the storehouse so that there will be food enough in my Temple; if you do, I will open up the windows of heaven for you and pour out a blessing so great you won't have room enough to take it in!

MALACHI 3:10, TLB

Give, and it will be given to you; good measure, pressed down, shaken together, running over, they will be poured into your lap. For by your standard of measure, it will be measured to you in return.

LUKE 6:38, NASB

So I say to you: Ask and it will be given to you; seek and you will find; knock and the door will be opened to you. For everyone who asks receives; he who seeks finds; and to him who knocks, the door will be opened.

LUKE 11:9-10, NIV

Yet he proved he is real by showing kindness, by giving you rain from heaven and crops at the right times, by giving you food and filling your hearts with joy.

ACTS 14:17, NCV

Command those who are rich in this present world not to be arrogant nor to put their hope in wealth, which is so uncertain, but to put their hope in God, who richly provides us with everything for our enjoyment.

1 TIMOTHY 6:17, NIV

CHAPTER
TWENTY-FOUR

GOD'S PROMISES OF HELP IN ADVERSITY

*God does not offer
us a way out of
the adversities of
life. He offers us
a way through,
and that makes all
the difference.*

W. T. PURKISER

I have told you these things, so that in me you may have peace. In this world you will have trouble. But take heart! I have overcome the world.

JOHN 16:33, NIV

The LORD defends those who suffer; he defends them in times of trouble.

PSALM 9:9, NCV

LORD, surely you see these cruel and evil things; look at them and do something. People in trouble look to you for help. You are the one who helps the orphans.

PSALM 10:14, NCV

God blesses those who are kind to the poor. He helps them out of their troubles.

PSALM 41:1, TLB

Call upon me in the day of trouble; I will deliver you, and you will honor me.

PSALM 50:15, NIV

The LORD is good, a refuge in times of trouble. He cares for those who trust in him.

NAHUM 1:7, NIV

We also have joy with our troubles, because we know that these troubles produce patience. And patience produces character, and character produces hope. And this hope will never disappoint us, because God has poured out his love to fill our hearts. He gave us his love through the Holy Spirit, whom God has given to us.

ROMANS 5:3-5, NCV

Blessed be the God and Father of our Lord Jesus Christ, the Father of mercies and God of all comfort, who comforts us in all our tribulation, that we may be able to comfort those who are in any trouble, with the comfort with which we ourselves are comforted by God.

2 CORINTHIANS 1:3-4, NKJV

My brothers and sisters, when you have many kinds of troubles, you should be full of joy, because you know that these troubles test your faith, and this will give you patience. Let your patience show itself perfectly in what you do. Then you will be perfect and complete and will have everything you need.

JAMES 1:2-4, NCV

CHAPTER TWENTY-FIVE

GOD'S PROMISES OF TRUTH

esus said, "If you abide in My word, then you are truly disciples of Mine; and you shall know the truth, and the truth shall make you free."

JOHN 8:31-32, NASB

The time is coming when the true worshipers will worship the Father in spirit and truth, and that time is here already. You see, the Father too is actively seeking such people to worship him.

JOHN 4:23-24, NCV

For the word of the LORD is right; and all his works are done in truth.

PSALM 33:4, KJV

And the Word became flesh, and dwelt among us, and we beheld His glory, glory as of the only begotten from the Father, full of grace and truth.

JOHN 1:14, NASB

For the law was given through Moses; grace and truth came through Jesus Christ.

JOHN 1:17, NIV

But he who does the truth comes to the light, that his deeds may be clearly seen, that they have been done in God.

JOHN 3:21, NKJV

This is good, and pleases God our Savior, who wants all men to be saved and to come to a knowledge of the truth.

1 TIMOTHY 2:3-4, NIV

God decided to give us life through the word of truth so we might be the most important of all the things he made.

JAMES 1:18, NCV

[Love] does not rejoice in unrighteousness, but rejoices with the truth.

1 CORINTHIANS 13:6, NASB

Jesus answered, "I am the way and the truth and the life. No one comes to the Father except through me."

JOHN 14:6, NIV

GOD'S PROMISES OF WISDOM

f any of you lacks wisdom, he should ask God, who gives generously to all without finding fault, and it will be given to him.

JAMES 1:5, NIV

My child, listen to what I say and remember what I command you. Listen carefully to wisdom; set your mind on understanding. Cry out for wisdom, and beg for understanding. Search for it like silver, and hunt for it like hidden treasure. Then you will understand respect for the LORD, and you will find that you know God. Only the LORD gives wisdom; he gives knowledge and understanding.

PROVERBS 2:1-6, NCV

Happy is the man who finds wisdom, and the man who gains understanding, for her proceeds are better than the profits of silver, and her gain better than fine gold. She is more precious than rubies; and all the things you may desire cannot compare with her.

PROVERBS 3:13-15, NKJV

Respect for the LORD will teach you wisdom. If you want to be honored, you must be humble.

PROVERBS 15:33, NCV

The LORD is exalted; for he dwelleth on high: he hath filled Zion with judgment and righteousness. And wisdom and knowledge shall be the stability of thy times, and strength of salvation: the fear of the LORD is his treasure.

ISAIAH 33:5-6, KJV

Praise God forever and ever, because he has wisdom and power. He changes the times and seasons of the year. He takes away the power of kings and gives their power to new kings. He gives wisdom to those who are wise and knowledge to those who understand.

DANIEL 2:20-21, NCV

For God gives those who please him wisdom, knowledge, and joy; but if a sinner becomes wealthy, God takes the wealth away from him and gives it to those who please him.

ECCLESIASTES 2:26, TLB

For I will give you words and wisdom that none of your adversaries will be able to resist or contradict.

LUKE 21:15, NIV

Who is wise and understanding among you? Let him show it by his good conduct that his works are done in the meekness of wisdom.

JAMES 3:13, NKJV

CHAPTER
TWENTY-SEVEN

GOD'S PROMISES OF VICTORIOUS LIVING

Triumphant Christians do not fight for victory, they celebrate a victory already won. The victorious life is Christ's business, not ours.

REGINALD WALLIS

I have fought the good fight, I have finished the race, I have kept the faith. Now there is in store for me the crown of righteousness, which the LORD, the righteous Judge, will award to me on that day—and not only to me, but also to all who have longed for his appearing.

2 TIMOTHY 4:7-8, NIV

The LORD your God goes with you, to fight for you against your enemies and to save you.

DEUTERONOMY 20:4, NCV

You have also given me the shield of Your salvation; your gentleness has made me great.

2 SAMUEL 22:36, NKJV

In all these things we are more than conquerors through him that loved us. For I am persuaded, that neither death, nor life, nor angels, nor principalities, nor powers, nor things present, nor things to come, nor height, nor depth, nor any other creature, shall be able to separate us from the love of God, which is in Christ Jesus our Lord.

ROMANS 8:37-39, KJV

You give us victory over our enemies, you put our adversaries to shame.

PSALM 44:7, NIV

He stores up sound wisdom for the upright; He is a shield to those who walk in integrity.

PROVERBS 2:7, NASB

"They will fight against you but will not overcome you, for I am with you and will rescue you," declares the LORD.

JEREMIAH 1:19, NIV

You are from God, little children, and have overcome them, because He who is in you is greater than the he who is in the world.

1 JOHN 4:4, NKJV

For our earthly bodies, the ones we have now that can die, must be transformed into heavenly bodies that cannot perish but will live forever. When this happens, then at last this Scripture will come true—"Death is swallowed up in victory." O death where then your victory? Where then your sting? How we thank God for all of this! It is he who makes us victorious through Jesus Christ our Lord.

1 CORINTHIANS 15:53-55, 57, TLB

CHAPTER TWENTY-EIGHT

GOD'S PROMISES OF INHERITANCE

 hatever you do, work at it with all your heart, as working for the Lord, not for men, since you know that you will receive an inheritance from the Lord as a reward. It is the Lord Christ you are serving.

COLOSSIANS 3:23-24 NIV

Ask of me, and I will make the nations your inheritance, the ends of the earth your possession.

PSALM 2:8 NIV

He who leads the upright along an evil path will fall into his own trap, but the blameless will receive a good inheritance.

PROVERBS 28:10 NIV

Instead of their shame my people will receive a double portion, and instead of disgrace they will rejoice in their inheritance; and so they will inherit a double portion in their land, and everlasting joy will be theirs.

ISAIAH 61:7 NIV

Then shall the King say unto them on his right hand,
Come, ye blessed of my Father, inherit the kingdom
prepared for you from the foundation of the world:

MATTHEW 25:34 KJV

Now, brethren, I commend you to God, and to the word
of his grace, which is able to build you up, and to give
you an inheritance among all them which are sanctified.

ACTS 20:32 KJV

You also were included in Christ when you heard the
word of truth, the gospel of your salvation. Having
believed, you were marked in him with a seal, the
promised Holy Spirit, who is a deposit guaranteeing our
inheritance until the redemption of those who are God's
possession — to the praise of his glory.

EPHESIANS 1:13-14 NIV

Blessed be the God and Father of our Lord Jesus Christ,
which according to his abundant mercy hath begotten
us again unto a lively hope by the resurrection of Jesus
Christ from the dead, to an inheritance incorruptible,
and undefiled, and that fadeth not away, reserved in
heaven for you.

I PETER 1:3-4 KJV

Dear friends, since we have these promises, let us purify ourselves and perfect our holiness out of reverence for God.

2 CORINTHIANS 7:1